THE WORDS OF
HARRY S TRUMAN

THE WORDS OF
HARRY S TRUMAN

★ ★ ★ ★

SELECTED BY
Robert J. Donovan

NEWMARKET PRESS
NEW YORK

First Edition
1 2 3 4 5 6 7 8 9 0 F/C

Library of Congress Cataloging in Publication Data

Truman, Harry S., 1884–1972.
  The words of Harry S Truman.

  Bibliography: p.
  Summary: A compilation of quotations from the speeches
and writings of our thirty-third President.
  1. United States—Politics and government—1945–
1953—Addresses, essays, lectures. [1. United States—
Politics and government—1945–1953—Addresses, essays,
lectures] I. Donovan, Robert J. II. Title.
  J82.D7 1984   973.918′092′4   84-18910
  ISBN 0-937858-48-X

Manufactured in the United States of America

Other volumes in the Newmarket *Words* series include
  The Words of Gandhi
  The Words of Martin Luther King, Jr.
  The Words of Albert Schweitzer

Quantity Purchases
*Companies, professional groups, clubs, and other organizations may
qualify for special terms when ordering quantities of this title. For
information, contact the Special Sales Department, Newmarket Press, 3
East 48th Street, New York, New York 10017. Phone (212) 832-3575.*

CONTENTS

INTRODUCTION
by Robert J. Donovan

As a recently assigned Washington correspondent for the old *New York Herald Tribune*, I saw President Harry S Truman for the first time in May 1947 at a White House Press conference. As was the custom then, my bureau chief introduced me to the president as a newcomer in town. I came away with several impressions, some of which were to change drastically before long.

My first impression was that Mr. Truman, as reporters usually referred to him, was a much less imposing figure than earlier presidents. As a child I had stood in Delaware Park in Buffalo, waving a flag at President Woodrow Wilson as he passed in an open Pierce Arrow. I have never forgotten the dignity of his appearance in a high silk hat and overcoat with a fur collar. As time went on, I frequently saw photographs of President Herbert Hoover, looking sedate in a high starched collar. Then, of course, came the years of often-dramatic pictures of President Franklin D. Roosevelt, especially late in the Second World War when he stood on the bridge of a cruiser or rode through the streets of New York, majestically wearing a long cape. President Truman, the first time I saw him, did not look majestic at all, though I noticed that he was very neatly, even a bit nattily, dressed, but not dressed for effect.

He replied to questions at the press conference in a staccato delivery: to the point, yet thin in commentary of a kind that would educate citizens reading his words.

Since no big stories were running that day, neither the questions nor the answers were particularly interesting, let alone memorable. I was pleased, though, that when President Truman talked to reporters face-to-face, his voice was deeper and more resonant than the Missouri twang I had heard when he read speeches on the radio. On the other hand, with his smoothed-down gray hair, thick glasses, solemn expression, and double-breasted blue suit and dark necktie, he struck me as quite colorless, which shows how wrong first impressions can be.

My most enduring recollection of that day, however, is that of President Truman's handshake: it was not just strong, it was athletic. The truth did not dawn on me until long afterward that the handshake was that of a then sixty-three-year-old man who for a dozen years of his young adult life had worked on a farm in his native Missouri, pitching hay, sowing beans, and plowing fields. Though many people did not seem to be conscious of the fact, Truman in his sixties was an unusually sturdy man.

Matching his physical sturdiness was a sturdiness of mind and temperament. This is not to imply that Harry Truman was an intellectual. He was simply a man of sound mind who was very much at ease with himself and secure in his family and forebears. Unlike some other modern presidents—Lyndon B. Johnson comes to mind—he was remarkably free of emotional hang-ups. Whereas certain of his critics, the early ones especially, thought he was too "little" a man for the presidency, in fact he was self-confident almost to a fault, tending to make some decisions too quickly, choosing a course without searching out the possible consequences. President Truman told the truth about himself when he said that he did his best each day and then stopped worrying and had a good night's sleep to prepare for the next day's tasks. He was not one to toss and turn. After ordering the relief of General of the Army Douglas A. MacArthur in 1951, he went to bed and to sleep even before the announcement was made, though he knew full well it would cause pandemonium.

The better I came to know it, the more astonishing the whole story of Truman's life and career was. A product of farms and small towns in Missouri, he completed high school and then worked at various jobs, mainly farming. In the First World War he went to France as a combat artillery officer. After the war, he and a friend opened a haberdashery in Kansas City, but it failed in the depression of 1920–1921. With the support of the Pendergast Democratic organization, Truman entered politics and was elected a commissioner of Jackson County, which included Kansas City and his home town of Independence. He was still a county commissioner at the age of fifty, when many men see the shadow of retirement coming. He had not the semblance of a national reputation. That was in 1934. In 1945 he was president of the United States—and at one of the great turning points in modern history. Truman had not been in the White House for five months before he had to decide whether to drop atomic bombs on Japan and how to respond to Stalin's intrusions into Poland and Eastern Europe and whether to send occupation troops into southern Korea and how to bring about the massive reconversion of the wartime economy of the United States to a peacetime economy. And these issues were only the beginning of a series of momentous decisions that were to exert a great impact on the history of the second half of the twentieth century.

The gap between Truman's being a county commissioner and president of the United States was filled by ten years as a United States senator from Missouri and

eighty-three days as vice-president under President
Franklin D. Roosevelt, beginning on January 20, 1945.
When Roosevelt ran for a fourth term in 1944, a split in
the Democratic party necessitated the choice of a com-
promise candidate for vice-president. Truman was the one
most acceptable to the conflicting factions, and although
he preferred to remain a senator, he bowed to the de-
mands of party loyalty. In his new capacity of vice-
president he was presiding over a routine session of the
Senate on April 12, 1945, when he was summoned to
the White House without explanation. Upon his arrival,
Eleanor Roosevelt said to him, "Harry, the president
is dead." At 7:09 that evening, Truman took the oath of
office, succeeding Roosevelt, who had died suddenly in
Warm Springs, Georgia.

For one who had not had a shred of experience in
the conduct of foreign affairs, Truman faced an awe-
some situation. The Second World War was at a climax.
The Allied nations in Europe were exhausted. Germany
and Japan were toppling. Old European empires were
collapsing. Civil war was brewing in China and Vietnam.
The Middle East was approaching the hostilities in
which Israel was to be born. Although devastated by war,
the Soviet Union under Stalin was rising as one of two
superpowers.

A critical fact about President Truman was that
he believed that the United States should exert strong
international leadership and not revert to isolationism,
as it did after the First World War. Such a viewpoint
aligned him with powerful elements in Congress, in
business and industry, in labor, in the universities, in
banking and investment houses, in the armed services,
and in the press. His advocacy of a strong international-
ist policy put him in accord not only with Rooseveltian
Democrats but with such Republicans as Thomas E.

Dewey, John Foster Dulles, and Henry L. Stimson. Despite differences on detail, Truman stood at the head of a powerful consensus favoring a dominant American role, moral leadership, support of capitalist interests, and prevention of Communist expansionism. That consensus determined the direction of postwar American foreign policy.

Even before Roosevelt died, disturbing differences were arising between the Western Allies and the Kremlin, centering on the make-up of the future Polish government, but radiating beyond that to various postwar questions. Then on April 12, 1945, the task of dealing with the conflicts suddenly fell into Truman's inexperienced hands. The symbols of his decisions are the Truman Doctrine, the Marshall Plan, the Berlin airlift, NATO, the Point Four program of technical assistance to underdeveloped countries, and the building of friendly ties with America's erstwhile enemies, Japan and West Germany.

In time, Stalin's pressures on Eastern Europe, the Black Sea Straits, and Iran convinced American policymakers that he was seeking to dominate the world. The Truman administration responded with a policy of containment of communism, first in Europe and later in the Far East—one expression of the Truman Doctrine. Truman believed that the security of the United States and Europe were indivisible. He undertook to unite and strengthen what became known as the North Atlantic community, which actually included the Mediterranean states of Italy, Greece, and Turkey as well as the Scandinavian countries.

The primary purpose of the Marshall Plan was to put the European nations on the road to economic recovery from the war, lest some of them succumb to communism. Even as the task was beginning, the Soviets shocked the West by seizing control of Czechoslovakia and creating an alarming challenge to the Allies by blockading Berlin. Western European leaders feared a possible Soviet attack on their countries. For psychological reasons and to provide a shield behind which the Europeans could tackle the task of economic recovery, Truman approved United States membership in the North Atlantic Treaty. The keystone was an agreement by the parties that an armed attack against one of them would be considered an attack on all. For the first time practically since George Washington's farewell address, a president had committed the United States to a permanent alliance outside the Western Hemisphere. In an accompanying, unprecedented step, Truman later dispatched American troops to Europe in peacetime. They are still there as part of NATO forces.

Truman was beset by worse difficulties in Asia. Before he took office, China was on the brink of civil war between the Communists and the Nationalists, who were supported by the United States. Through General George C. Marshall, Truman tried to mediate the conflict, but without success. In the strife that followed, the Communists seized control of China. In the United States, Republicans found a hot issue in blaming Truman for the "loss" of China, and they pressed it so hard his leadership was damaged.

Another crisis confronted him in Korea. In carrying out a policy that had originated in the Roosevelt administration, Truman sent occupying forces into southern Korea after Japan's surrender in 1945. At the same time, the Soviets occupied northern Korea. The 38th parallel divided the two forces. In the south the Americans fostered a right-wing regime; in the north the Soviets established a Communist regime. Each regime aspired to rule all of Korea.

On June 25, 1950, Soviet-backed North Korea invaded American-supported South Korea. Truman sent troops to South Korea under General MacArthur to repel the invaders. After hard fighting, MacArthur succeeded in driving the Communist forces back across the 38th parallel in September 1950. Under public pressure and on the advice of his advisers, Truman ordered MacArthur's forces across the parallel to pursue and destroy the remnants of the North Korean army in preparation for the unification of Korea as a free and independent nation. The result was disaster.

Fearful for its own security, Communist China poured three hundred thousand troops into North Korea and drove MacArthur's forces back into South Korea. MacArthur wanted American bombers dispatched to destroy all of China's industrial centers. He also wanted the United States to blockade the Chinese coast. Believing that such acts of war might lead to a third world war, Truman insisted on limiting the fighting to Korea. MacArthur dissented and continued to dissent until Truman relieved him for insubordination, inviting violent criticism from conservative Republicans and right-wing elements.

Concerned that the Chinese Communists might sweep into Southeast Asia, Truman intervened in another civil war, this one in Vietnam in 1950. He granted diplomatic recognition to an anti-Communist puppet regime in South Vietnam and sent money and a military mission to help it in a futile effort to defeat the Nationalist-Communist revolutionaries led by Ho Chi Minh. Thus, on a small scale, the United States became involved at that time in the developing tragedy in Vietnam.

In domestic affairs Truman engaged in stormy conflicts with the Republican-controlled Eightieth Congress of 1947–1948; with the China lobby, which battled for more aid to the Chinese Nationalists in China's civil war; and with Senator Joseph R. McCarthy, who went on a rampage, baselessly accusing the Truman administration of harboring Communists. The main thrust of Truman's domestic policy was preserving and extending the New Deal, carrying forward social programs in the areas of housing, employment, and social security, among others. He did succeed in preserving the main Roosevelt reforms against partisan attack. But a coalition of Republicans and Southern Democrats in Congress blocked Truman's main efforts to extend the New Deal under the name of the Fair Deal.

The Second World War lent great impetus to the movement to end racial discrimination in the United States, and Truman was caught in the middle of it. He came from a Jim Crow state and had always had to pick his way cautiously through the turmoil of the civil rights issue. On the other hand, he felt strongly that blacks were entitled to their constitutional rights and that the time had come for the nation to act accordingly. Public opinion, however, lagged on the issue, and powerful Southern forces were arrayed in Congress to block reforms. On February 2, 1948, Truman submitted to Congress the first comprehensive civil rights program ever proposed by a president. Including recommendations for a voting rights measure, it proposed a large part of the agenda for the civil rights revolution of the 1960s and 1970s. Nevertheless, Congress refused to touch it during Truman's presidency. In one notable achievement, however, he issued an executive order to desegregate the armed forces.

President Truman's defeat of Governor Thomas E. Dewey in the 1948 election, which the pollsters and nearly everyone else had conceded in advance to Dewey, was Truman's most exciting hour. His decision that left the most enduring controversy was announced by him on August 6, 1945: "Sixteen hours ago an American airplane dropped one bomb on Hiroshima. . . . It is an atomic bomb." It is easier to blame Truman than to explore the many reasons why he went ahead with the plans to use the weapon, which had been under consideration since before he became president. His basic rationale was that by ending the war quickly, a net saving would be realized in Japanese as well as American lives lost. That reasoning may well have been correct. Still, the introduction of nuclear weapons was a step now widely condemned.

On the whole, however, the passage of time has been kind to Truman. Unquestionably, the simple, straightforward, spirited man of Independence is, in 1984, his centennial year, one of the best liked and most respected of all American presidents.

★ ★ ★

I covered the Truman story to the end of his term, and rode back to Independence with Harry and Bess aboard the Baltimore & Ohio's National Limited. The train departed Washington several hours after Dwight D. Eisenhower had been inaugurated as president on January 20, 1953. Democrats at the departure from Union Station sang "Auld Lang Syne." In a happy mood, the retired president said he would live to be one hundred years, a goal of which he fell short by twelve years, although Bess made it to ninety-seven.

The trip home was a rollicking affair. While the Trumans occupied the presidential car at the rear of the train, Mr. Truman, a private citizen again, persisted in wandering through the other twelve cars. "By golly, he's right here!" exclaimed a woman as he appeared in one car. "My stars alive!" gasped another woman passenger in the next car forward.

At Cincinnati the next morning, he caused a commotion in the station by going to the newsstand to buy a couple of papers. At other stops he talked to crowds from the rear platform of his car, just as he had in the 1948 whistle-stop campaign. During a stop at Vincennes, Indiana, he took a stroll forward on the platform to see the locomotive. "Glad to see you, old boy," cried the engineer. "God bless you and your family." At Washington, Indiana, an eleven-year-old boy hit Truman for fifty cents for a ticket to a Parents-Teachers Association card party, while a spectator told Mr. Truman, "You are the man with the greatest personality in the U.S." While chatting with the crowd there, the former president was asked if he was going to take life easy now.

"It's not hard work that gets a man into trouble— it's the lack of it," he replied. "When a fellow has nothing to do, he gets into devilment."

Strolling through Pullman cars, Truman would sometimes poke his head into the open door of compartments, sending occupants into fits of astonishment. But in one instance a couple did not recognize him at all. "Things are getting back to normal when that happens," Truman observed wryly.

How quickly indeed power passes. At a luncheon at Dean Acheson's house before the train departed Union Station, Truman had remarked to a friend: "Two hours ago I could have said five words and been quoted in fifteen minutes in every capital in the world. Now I could talk for two hours and nobody would give a damn." Mingling with the passengers on the way to the Midwest,

Truman could easily have been mistaken for just another traveler. In a way, that suggests why he has such a marked appeal to Americans a generation later: eight years in the White House and no airs, no pretensions, no wealth accumulated through political power and prestige, no hypocrisy, no vain boasts. He had simply said in his farewell address, "I tried to give it everything that was in me."

POLITICS
AND LEADERSHIP

★ ★ ★

"The buck stops here."

"I wonder how far Moses would have gone if he'd taken a poll in Egypt? What would Jesus Christ have preached if he'd taken a poll in Israel? Where would the Reformation have gone if Martin Luther had taken a poll? It isn't polls or public opinion at the moment that counts. It is right and wrong and leadership—men with fortitude, honesty, and a belief in the right that makes epochs in the history of the world."

"Within the first few months I discovered that being a president is like riding a tiger. A man has to keep on riding or be swallowed."

"I do not know of any easy way to be president. It is more than a full-time job, and the relaxations are few."

"The president of Princeton University spoke of crises a while ago. He should try sitting in my chair for about an hour and a half!"

"My political philosophy is based on the Sermon on the Mount. And it is the hardest thing in the world for any man to live up to. If you haven't read it lately, I would advise you to go home tonight and read it. It will do you a lot of good."

"Do you know what makes a leader? It's a man or woman who can persuade people to do what they ought to do—and which they sometimes don't do—without being persuaded. They must also have the ability to persuade people to do what they do not want to do and like it. That, in my opinion, is the best definition of leadership."

"The president's duties. . . .

"He has more duties and powers than a Roman emperor, a general, a Hitler or a Mussolini; but he never uses those powers or prerogatives, because he is a democrat (with a small *d*) and because he believes in the Magna Carta and the Bill of Rights. But first he believes in the XXth Chapter of Exodus, the Vth Chapter of Deuteronomy, and the V, VI & VIIth chapters of the Gospel according to St. Matthew.

"He should be a Cincinnatus, Marcus Aurelius Antoninus, a Cato, Washington, Jefferson and Jackson all in one. I fear that there is no such man. But if we have one who tries to do what is right because it is right, the greatest republic in the history of the world will survive."

"One of the results of [our] system is that it gives the president a good many hot potatoes to handle. . . . The president gets a lot of hot potatoes from every direction anyhow, and a man who can't handle them has no business in that job. That makes me think of a saying I used to hear from my old friend and colleague on the Jackson County Court. He said, 'Harry, if you can't stand the heat, you better get out of the kitchen.' "

"Ultimately, no president can master his responsibilities, save as his fellow citizens—indeed the whole people—comprehend the challenge of our times and move, with him, to meet it."

"The world today [1947] looks to us for leadership.

"The force of events makes it necessary that we assume that role.

"This is a critical period of our national life. The process of adapting ourselves to the new concept of our world responsibility is naturally a difficult and painful one. The cost is necessarily great.

"It is not our nature to shirk our obligations. We have a heritage that constitutes the greatest resources of this nation. I call it the spirit and character of the American people.

"We are the people who gave the world George Washington, Thomas Jefferson, Andrew Jackson, Abraham Lincoln, Woodrow Wilson, and Franklin D. Roosevelt.

"We are a people who not only cherish freedom and defend it, if need be with our lives, but we also recognize the right of other men and other nations to share it.

"While the struggle for the rights of man goes forward in other parts of the world, the free peoples of America cannot look on with easy detachment, with indifference to the outcome."

"No government is perfect. One of the chief virtues of a democracy, however, is that its defects are always visible and under democratic processes can be pointed out and corrected."

"At the present moment in world history nearly every nation must choose between alternative ways of life. The choice is too often not a free one.

"One way of life is based upon the will of the majority and is distinguished by free institutions, representative government, free elections, guarantees of individual liberty, freedom of speech and religion, and freedom from political oppression.

"The second way of life is based upon the will of a minority forcibly imposed upon the majority. It relies upon terror and oppression, a controlled press and radio, fixed elections, and the suppression of personal freedoms.

"I believe that it must be the policy of the United States to support free peoples who are resisting subjugation by armed minorities or by outside pressures."*

*This was the statement that became known as the Truman Doctrine.

"Whenever a president is in office everybody has a right to throw mudballs at him if they want to. . . . If he can't dodge them, it's too bad. But in foreign policy it is necessary that this country present a solid front to the world on the policy which we want to pursue."

"You know, I was a member of the Senate for ten years, and I found that it didn't pay to fall out with a fellow because he was against you one time. The next time, when you needed him worse, he might be along on your side.

"We must also bear in mind [1946] that everybody's tired—everybody's tired—everybody wants to quit. . . . It's difficult to find people who want to expend any energy now—they are all war-weary.

"The Congress hasn't been home since 1939 for any length of time. The last time I was at home was in September [or] August '39, and then Hitler went into Poland, and Congress has been constantly in session ever since then. Those men are just as tired as the soldiers . . . and all the rest of the people who fought the war here in Washington. Sometimes they get a little cranky with the president. But I am looking forward to the time when it will work out all right."

"It has been my experience in public life that there are few problems which cannot be worked out, if we make a real effort to understand the other fellow's point of view, and if we try to find a solution on the basis of give-and-take, of fairness to both sides."

"In my opinion eight years as president is enough and sometimes too much for any man to serve. . . . There is a lure in power. It can get into a man's blood just as gambling and lust for money have been known to do."

"The Democratic Party cannot exist as a 'me too' party. It must exist for all the people rich and poor, privileged and underprivileged. It must be ready to see justice done to those who can't hire expensive representatives to look after their welfare in Washington.

"Only the president can do that. He must be a fighter and one whose heart is in the general welfare."

"If you've done the best you can—if you have done what you have to do—there is no use worrying about it, because nothing can change it, and to be in a position of leadership . . . you have to give thought to what's going to happen the next day and you have to be fresh for . . . what you have to do the next day. What you're *going* to do is more important than what you have done."

"If you don't like people, you hadn't ought to be in politics at all."

"It hasn't been easy to make the New Deal and the Fair Deal a success. We have had a lot of opposition. Sometimes representatives of special privilege have been able to hold us back. . . .

"Most of the special privilege boys are better off than they have ever been in their lives, but they still say that the New Deal and the Fair Deal are taking the country to the dogs and to ruin. . . . It's a wonderful ruin, and I'm glad to be a part of it.

"That's what they have been saying for eighteen years, and all the time they have been getting better off—been getting more prosperous all the time.

"We have economic fossils today who want the profits of 1951 with the wages and hours of McKinley's first term.

"These antipeople have been wrong so constantly for so long that it makes you wonder how they can keep it up. But they do."

"The power of the Kremlin [1951] is more effective, more violent, more far-reaching than the power of the bloodiest of the czars, or the power of Genghis Khan, Tamerlane, Louis XIV, Charles V of Spain, or the power of any other of the tyrants of the past.

"Today, the tyrant can uproot and liquidate whole classes of people and entire nations. The death camps of Hitler Germany or of modern Siberia demonstrate that the unrestrained power of the government can be a greater evil in our modern civilization than it ever was in ancient times.

"The only guarantee against such a society of fear and cruelty is the principle that the government is not above the law. Our Declaration of Independence and our Constitution proclaim that the government is subject to the fundamental law. . . .

"Acting under our Constitution, we have been able to solve the problems which have driven other countries into revolution."

"One of the major lessons of recent world history is that free and vital trade unions are a strong bulwark against the growth of totalitarian movements. We must, therefore, be everlastingly alert that in striking at union abuses, we do not destroy contributions which unions make to our democratic strength."

"I am convinced that if labor and management will approach each other with the realization that they have a common goal and with the determination to compose their differences in their own long-range interest, it will not be long before we have put industrial strife behind us. Labor is the best customer that management has, and management is the source of labor's livelihood. Both are wholly dependent upon each other, and the country in turn is dependent upon both of them."

"I do not understand a mind which sees a gracious beneficence in spending money to slay and maim human beings in almost unimaginable [numbers] and deprecates the expenditure of a smaller sum to patch up the ills of erring mankind."

"On all sides [1948] there is heartening evidence of great energy—of capacity for economic development and even more important, capacity for spiritual growth. But accompanying this great activity there are equally great questions, great anxieties, and great aspirations. They represent the concern of an enlightened people that conditions should be arranged so as to make life more worthwhile.

"We must devote ourselves to finding answers to these anxieties and aspirations. We seek answers which will embody the moral and spiritual elements of tolerance, unselfishness, and brotherhood, upon which true freedom and opportunity must rest."

"Efficiency alone is not enough in government. . . . There must be life and hope in government. . . . Hitler learned that efficiency without justice is a vain thing. Democracy does not work that way. Democracy is a matter of faith—a faith in the soul of man, a faith in human rights. . . . Faith is much more than efficiency. Faith gives value to all things. Without faith, the people perish."

"I have never been able to understand all the fuss some people make about government wanting to do something to improve and protect the health of the people."

"The presidency of the United States carries with it a responsibility so personal as to be without parallel.
"Very few are ever authorized to speak for the president. No one can make decisions for him. No one can know all the processes and stages of his thinking in making important decisions. Even those closest to him, even members of his immediate family, never know all the reasons he does certain things and why he comes to certain conclusions. To be president of the United States is to be lonely, very lonely at times of great decisions."

"Our government cannot function properly unless the president is master in his own house and unless the executive departments and agencies of government, including the armed forces, are responsible only to the president."

"The very fact that he's the chief executive makes it necessary for the president to understand the nation, its relations with other nations, and its relations to the people here at home. If he does that, he's well on the way to accomplishing the purposes for which he was elected. He's got to understand people. In other words, he's got to be a good politician, and a politician is a man who understands government. I'm proud to be called a politician."

"There isn't any doubt but what a woman would make a good president. They make good senators, good members of the House of Representatives, and have held other important offices in the government of the United States."

"My debt to history is one which cannot be calculated. . . .* The leader of any country, in order to assume his responsibilities . . . must know the history of not only his own country but of all other great countries, and . . . he must make the effort to apply this knowledge to the decisions that have to be made for the welfare of all the people."

*Truman was an indefatigable reader of history all his life.

"When the American people, as a people, understand the circumstances and the truth, the demagogues don't last very long in this country."

"I intend to . . . act in this office as the agent of the American people, without regard to my personal political fortunes. . . .

"As president of the United States, I am guided by a simple formula: to do in all cases, from day to day, without regard to narrow political considerations, what seems to me to be best for the welfare of all our people."

AN ORDINARY MAN

★ ★ ★

"I don't believe in anti-anything. A man has to have a program; you have to be for something, otherwise you will never get anywhere."

"I don't care what your politics are, I don't care what you believe politically, and I don't care what your religion is, as long as you live by it and act by it. But you must watch out for these people who make mountains out of something that doesn't exist—not even a molehill! ... The best way to handle them is to ridicule them. You know, there's no stuffed shirt that can stand ridicule. When you stick a pin in that stuffed shirt and let the air out, he's through!"

"You don't get any double-talk from me. I'm either for something or against it, and you know. You know what I stand for."

"I am sure that right down in your heart you know that the ordinary man is the backbone of any country—particularly is that true of a republic—and what I am trying to eliminate is the fringe at each end of the situation. I think small business, the small farmer, the small corporations are the backbone of any free society and when there are too many people on relief and too few people at the top who control the wealth of the country then we must look out."

"As you know, I speak plainly sometimes—in fact, I speak bluntly sometimes and I am going to speak plainly and bluntly today."

"I heard a fellow tell a story about how he felt when he had to make speeches. He said when he had to make a speech, he felt like the fellow who was at the funeral of his wife, and the undertaker had asked him if he would ride down to the cemetery in the same car with his mother-in-law. He said, 'Well, I can do it, but it's just going to spoil the whole day for me.' "

"Now Missouri has had a number of notorious characters. The three, I guess, most notorious are Mark Twain, Jesse James, and me. Mark and Jesse are dead and I have to fill in for them, so here I am."

"I tried to get into military service before I was twenty-one, but could not do so because my mother and father were reconstructed Southerners, and they were afraid I would have to wear a blue uniform."

"My favorite animal is the mule. He has more sense than a horse. He knows when to stop eating— and when to stop working."

"Some of the presidents were great and some of them weren't. I can say that because I wasn't one of the great presidents, but I had a good time trying to be one, I can tell you that."

To reporters, on April 13, 1945, Truman's first
full day as President:
"Boys, if you ever pray, pray for me now. I
don't know whether you fellows ever had a load of
hay fall on you, but when they told me yesterday
what had happened, I felt like the moon, the stars,
and all the planets had fallen on me."

"Do your duty, and history will do you justice."

"I am not in favor of erecting memorials to
people who are living. I think it bad business because a person may do something before he dies
that will make the people want to tear the memo-
rial down."

To his daughter, Margaret:
"Your dad will never be reckoned among the
great. But you can be sure he did his level best and
gave all he had to his country. There is an epi-
taph in Boot Hill Cemetery in Tombstone, Arizona,
which reads, 'Here lies Jack Williams; he done his
damnedest.' What more can a person do?"

HUMAN RIGHTS

★ ★ ★

"The American people stand firm in the faith which has inspired this nation from the beginning. We believe that all men have a right to equal justice under the law and equal opportunity to share in the common good. We believe that all men have a right to freedom of thought and opportunity. . . . From this faith we will not be moved."

"We are living in a time [1947] of profound and swiftly moving change. We see colonial peoples moving toward their independence. It is a process that we, as Americans, can understand and sympathize with, since it parallels our own struggle for independence. We, as Americans, will want to supply guidance and help wherever we can. One way in which we can help is to set an example of a nation in which people of different origins work peacefully and successfully alongside one another. . . . When we fail to live together in peace, the failure touches not us, as Americans, alone, but the cause of democracy itself in the whole world."

"We often hear it said that spiritual values are indestructible, but I think it should be said that they are indestructible only so long as men are ready and willing to take action to preserve them."

"It is my deep conviction that we have reached a turning point in the long history of our country's efforts to guarantee freedom and equality to all our citizens. Recent events in the United States and abroad have made us realize that it is more important today than ever before to ensure that all Americans enjoy these rights.

"When I say all Americans I mean all Americans.

"The civil rights laws written in the early years of our Republic and the traditions which have been built upon them are precious to us. Those laws were drawn up with the memory fresh in men's minds of the tyranny of an absentee government. They were written to protect the citizen against any possible tyrannical act by the new government in this country.

"But we cannot be content with a civil liberties program which emphasizes only the need of protection against the possibility of tyranny by the government. We cannot stop there.

"We must keep moving forward with new concepts of civil rights to safeguard our heritage. The extension of civil rights today means not protection of the people *against* the government, but protection of the people *by* the government.

"We must make the federal government a friendly, vigilant defender of the rights and equalities of all Americans. And again, I mean all Americans.

"As Americans, we believe that every man should be free to live his life as he wishes. He should be limited only by his responsibility to his fellow countrymen. If this freedom is to be more than a dream, each man must be guaranteed equality of opportunity. The only limit to an American's achievement should be his ability, his industry, and his character. . . .

"Our immediate task is to remove the last remnants of the barriers which stand between millions of our citizens and their birthright. There is no justifiable reason for discrimination because of ancestry or religion or race or color.

"We must not tolerate such limitations on the freedom of any of our people and on their enjoyment of basic rights which every citizen in a truly democratic society must possess.

"Every man should have the right to a decent home, the right to an education, the right to adequate medical care, the right to a worthwhile job . . . and the right to a fair trial in a fair court."

"Any denial of human rights is a denial of the basic beliefs of democracy."

"Under the Constitution, the right of all properly qualified citizens to vote is beyond question. Yet the exercise of this right is still subject to interference. Some individuals are prevented from voting by isolated actions of intimidation. Some whole groups are prevented by outmoded policies prevailing in certain states or communities.

"We need stronger statutory protection of the right to vote. . . .

"Requirements for the payment of poll taxes also interfere with the right to vote. . . . I believe the Congress should enact measures ensuring that the right to vote in elections for federal officers shall not be contingent upon payment of taxes. . . .

"I urge the Congress to prohibit discrimination and segregation in the use of interstate transportation facilities. . . .

"If we wish to inspire the peoples of the world whose freedom is in jeopardy, if we wish to restore hope to those who have already lost their civil liberties, if we wish to fulfill the promise that is ours, we must correct the remaining imperfections in our practice of democracy.

"We know the way. We need only the will."

"During the recent war and in the years since its close we have made much progress toward the equality of opportunity in our armed services without regard to race, color, religion, or national origin. I have instructed the secretary of defense to take steps to have the remaining instances of discrimination in the armed services eliminated as rapidly as possible."

"Eventually, we are going to have an America in which freedom and opportunity are the same for everyone. . . . We Americans have a democratic way of acting when our freedoms are threatened. . . .

"Today [1948] the democratic way of life is being challenged all over the world. Democracy's answer to the challenge of totalitarianism is its promise of equal rights and equal opportunity for all mankind."

"We do not believe that men exist merely to strengthen the state or to be cogs in the economic machine. We do believe that governments are created to serve the people and that economic systems exist to minister to their wants. We have a profound devotion to the welfare and rights of the individual as a human being."

"The States' Rights Democrats [or Dixiecrats, who walked out of the Democratic National Convention in Philadelphia in 1948 over adoption of a liberal civil rights plank] claimed that this was not a bolt from the Democratic party. They said they represented the true Democrats of the Southland. It was a bolt. It was also a manifestation of prejudice. I had seen at first hand a similar reaction in 1928, when Al Smith ran for the presidency on the Democratic ticket. I was very active in Jackson County [Missouri] politics at that time and did everything I could to carry the county for him. Still, because of anti-Catholic prejudice, our traditionally Democratic county voted Smith down by thirty thousand votes. Because of the success of that prejudice the belief was then stated that no Catholic, Jew, or Negro could ever hold high public office again. That was twenty-five years ago, and the prejudice has now become much less apparent, although it has yet to be overcome. Hitler's persecution of the Jews did much to awaken Americans to the dangerous extremes to which prejudice can be carried if allowed to control government actions.

"I never did believe that the great mass of Southerners had the same viewpoint as the minority Dixiecrat contingent. I was raised amidst some violently prejudiced Southerners myself, and I believe the vast majority of good Southerners understand that the blind prejudices of past generations cannot continue in a free republic. Much progress in civil rights has been made voluntarily by the South itself."

"The abundance we enjoy [in America] was created out of the riches of the soil and out of the labor of the men who work it and, above all, out of American faith. This faith has enabled people from many lands to come together, to live in peace, and to learn to respect each other as individuals.

"We are a diverse people, and in this diversity we have great strength. We have room for differences and room for disagreement. Part of our respect for the dignity of the human being is the respect for his right to be different. That means different in background, different in his beliefs, different in his customs, different in his name, and different in his religion."

"People are very much wrought up about the Communist 'bugaboo' but I am of the opinion that the country is perfectly safe so far as communism is concerned—we have far too many sane people. Our government is made for the welfare of the people and I don't believe there will ever come a time when anyone will really want to overturn it."

"Our system of justice. . . . protects [the citizen] in the assertion of his rights even against his own government."

"The American people are rightly concerned in these days [1948] about the attack on our ideals by international communism. . . . Some people think you can combat communism by outlawing the Communist party.

"It seems to me that such proposals miss the point entirely. You cannot stop the spread of an idea by passing a law against it. You cannot stamp out communism by driving it underground. You can prevent communism by more and better democracy.

"As far as the United States is concerned, the menace of communism is not the activities of a few foreign agents or the political activities of a few isolated individuals. The menace of communism lies primarily in those areas of American life where the promise of democracy remains unfulfilled."

"I am going to tell you how we are *not* going to fight communism. We are not going to transform our . . . FBI into a Gestapo secret police. That is what some people would like to do. We are not going to try to control what our people read and say and think. We are not going to turn the United States into a right-wing totalitarian country in order to deal with a left-wing totalitarian threat. . . . We are going to keep the Bill of Rights on the books."

"Soon after our government began functioning under the Constitution, there was enacted, in 1798, the group of legislative actions known as the Alien and Sedition Laws. These laws were ostensibly designed to prevent activities which would undermine the nation's safety and independence. But in fact they were broad enough—and were used—to imprison many leading citizens, including a member of Congress, who expressed disagreement with the policies of the administration then in office.*

"That experience taught us a great lesson: that extreme and arbitrary security measures strike at the very heart of our free society and that we must be eternally vigilant against those who would undermine freedom in the name of security."

"It is a tribute to the strong faith and common sense of our people that we have never for long been misled by the hysterical cries of those who would suppress our constitutional freedoms."

*The objectionable features of the laws soon were repealed or allowed to expire.

"Laws forbidding dissent do not prevent subversive activities; they merely drive them into more secret and more dangerous channels. Police states are not secure; their history is marked by successive purges and growing concentration camps, as their governments strike out blindly in fear of violent revolt. Once a government is committed to the principle of silencing the voice of opposition, it has only one way to go, and that is down the path of increasingly repressive measures, until it becomes a source of terror to all its citizens and creates a country where everyone lives in fear.

"We must, therefore, be on our guard against extremists who urge us to adopt police state methods. Such persons advocate breaking down the guarantees of the Bill of Rights in order to get at the Communists. They forget that if the Bill of Rights were to be broken down, all groups, even the most conservative, would be in danger from the arbitrary power of government."

GIVING 'EM HELL

★ ★ ★

"I'll mow 'em down, Alben, and I'll give 'em hell."*

"We discussed . . . [the] Supreme Commander [in the Far East] and what to do with Mr. Prima Donna, Brass Hat, Five Star MacArthur. He's worse than the Cabots and the Lodges—they at least talked with one another before they told God what to do. Mac tells God right off. It is a very great pity we have to have stuffed shirts like that in key positions. . . .

*President Truman's trainside rejoinder to the urging of his Democratic running mate in the 1948 campaign, Senator Alben W. Barkley of Kentucky. As the president was departing Union Station in Washington on a transcontinental whistle-stop trip, Barkley admonished, "Go out there and mow 'em down." Truman's rejoinder established the generic phrase that has been used to describe his celebrated brickbats and animadversions, on and off the campaign trail.

"Don't see how a country can produce such men as Robert E. Lee, John J. Pershing, Eisenhower, and Bradley and at the same time produce Custers, Pattons, and MacArthurs."

On relieving MacArthur of his command in Korea in 1951:
"I was sorry to have to reach a parting of the way with the big man in Asia, but he asked for it and I had to give it to him."

"It seems that every man in the White House [has been] tortured and bedeviled by the so-called free press. They were lied about, misrepresented, and actually libeled, and they had to take it and do nothing.

"The old S.O.B. who owned and edited the *St. Louis Post-Dispatch* and the *New York World** was in my opinion the meanest character assassin in the whole history of liars who have controlled newspapers—and that includes old man Hearst† and Bertie McCormick!"‡

Joseph Pulitzer
†*William Randolph Hearst*
‡*Colonel Robert McCormick, publisher of the* Chicago Tribune

"Don't worry about what *Life, Time,* or any other Luce (loose) publication may say about you....

"It seems to be the objective of such publications . . . along with *Look, Newsweek, Colliers, Saturday Evening Post,* and most of the big city newspapers to misrepresent and belittle [Truman]."

"I had thought that pictures and the radio would cure the news liars—but they—the liars—have taken over both.

"[Drew] Pearson, [Walter] Winchell, and local scavengers paid by such stations as WGN and WDAF make it impossible for listeners to get the facts.

"When I am finished here maybe I'll do it myself. I'll make a bet however that hell has become untenable for the devil since old Pulitzer, Horace Greeley, Charles Dana, the old copperhead Bill Nelson* and William Allen White arrived."

"If they want to ask me some impudent questions, I'll try to give them some impudent answers."

William R. Nelson of the Kansas City Star

"Whenever the press quits abusing me, I know I'm in the wrong pew."

"Mr. [Paul] Hume: I've just read your lousy review of Margaret's concert [in the *Washington Post* of December 6, 1950]. I've come to the conclusion that you are an 'eight ulcer man on four ulcer pay.'

"It seems to me that you are a frustrated old man [Hume was thirty-four] who wishes he could have been successful. When you write such poppy-cock as was in the back section of the paper you work for it shows conclusively that you're off the beam and at least four of your ulcers are at work.

"Someday I hope to meet you. When that happens you'll need a new nose, a lot of beefsteak for black eyes, and perhaps a supporter below!"

On the Roosevelts:
"I don't believe the USA wants any more fakers—Teddy and Franklin are enough."

"The cries from reactionary quarters after the [1948] State of the Union Message only prove the truth of my statement that some people are afraid to look ahead. These men who live in the past remind me of a toy I'm sure all of you have seen. The toy is a small wooden bird called the 'Floogie Bird.' Around the Floogie Bird's neck is a label reading: 'I fly backwards. I don't care where I'm going. I just want to see where I've been.' These backward-looking men refuse to see where courageous leadership can take this nation in the years that lie ahead."

"I asked the Congress last November [1947] ... to restore federal controls to the president so he could in his discretion hold down the cost of living to the common, everyday man. This Eightieth [Republican-controlled] Congress has not seen fit to take any action. . . . I am hoping that when we get a new Congress—and we are going to get one this fall [1948]—maybe we'll get one that will work in the interests of the common people and not the interests of the men who have all the money. Bear that in mind carefully."

"In the Eightieth Congress the chairmen were the Republicans who have been in Congress for the longest period of time. They are a bunch of old mossbacks.* They are living back in 1890, and they tried to make that Congress act like 1890—and they succeeded pretty well."

To the people of Bremerton, Washington, June 10, 1948:

"You know, this Congress is interested in the welfare of the better classes. They are not interested in the welfare of the common, everyday man. They said if we lifted price controls and things of that sort, business would take care of prices. Well, business has taken care of prices—for the welfare and the benefit of the fellows at the top. The poor man is having to pay out all his money for rent and for clothing and for food at prices that are certainly outrageous."

Voice: "Pour it on, Harry!"

"I'm going to. I'm going to!"

*The way the official White House stenographer mistakenly heard Truman, the reference to the Republican chairmen came out in the original transcript as "a bunch of old moth bags."

"I have been asking the Congress to broaden the base of Social Security.... Well, you know how Congress has broadened the base? ... They have just taken 750,000 people off Social Security and sent me a bill to that effect and tied a rider to it, increasing old-age assistance, hoping that I would take that bait and let them get away [with] wrecking Social Security.

"I didn't do it. I vetoed that bill this morning and I told the Congress that if it would pass the [bill] in proper form, I would be happy to sign it. And they have plenty of time to pass it in proper form. Don't think they haven't."

"I hope you will join me in this crusade to keep the country from going to the dogs."

"The Republicans ... put a dangerous weapon into the hands of the big corporations in the shape of the Taft-Hartley law which I vetoed but which was passed over my veto.... And you [members of the AFL and CIO] and I know that the Taft-Hartley law is only a foretaste of what you will get if [in 1948] the Republican reaction is allowed to continue to grow.

"If you let the Republican administration reactionaries get complete control of this government, the position of labor will be so greatly weakened that I would fear not only for the wages and living standards of the American workingman but even for our democratic institutions and free enterprise.

"Remember that the reactionary of today is a shrewd man. He is in many ways much shrewder than the reactionaries of the '20s. He is a man with a calculating machine where his heart ought to be. He has learned a great deal about how to get his way by observing demagogues and reactionaries in other countries. And now he has many able allies in the press and on the radio.

"If you place the government of this country under the control of those who hate labor, who can you blame if measures are thereafter adopted to destroy the powers, prestige, and earning power of labor. . . . Make no mistake, you are face-to-face with a struggle to preserve the very foundations of your rights and your standards of living."

"The Republicans favor a minimum wage—the smaller the minimum the better."

"You [people of Spokane, Washington] are not going to get those [flood control] projects as long as you have a Congress that believes in the theory of Daniel Webster: that the West is no good and there is no use wasting money on it. There are still men in the Congress who are following Daniel Webster, and they are the chairmen of the key committees which make these appropriations.

"If you don't do something about that [on election day, 1948], you don't deserve to have anything, that's all I can say to you. . . .

"I helped to write that [liberal 1944 Democratic] platform. I am trying to carry out that platform, but I am not getting very much help from this Congress.

"That's partly your fault. . . . In the [congressional] election of 1946 you believed all the lies that were published about your president [Truman]. And two-thirds of you didn't even go out and vote. Look what the other third gave you! You deserved it.

"Now, if you let that sort of situation continue—you have got a chance to remedy it this fall—I won't have any sympathy with you. You will get just what you deserve."

"Of course, we don't know what [Dewey] means by unity because he won't tell the country where he stands on any of the issues. . . . He doesn't dare tell the country what the real plans of the Republican party are. He's afraid that if he says anything, he'll give the whole show away."

"Apparently, I have offended the Republican gentleman who wants to be president. . . . Republicans don't like people who talk about depressions. You can hardly blame them for that. You remember the old saying: Don't talk about rope in the house where somebody has been hanged."

"This is your fight. I am only waking you up to the fact that it is your fight. You better get out and help me win this fight, or you're going to be the loser, not I."

"We're going to lick 'em just as sure as you stand there!"

To an assemblage of farmers in Dexter, Iowa, on September 18, 1948:

"The Wall Street reactionaries are not satisfied with being rich. They want to increase their power and privilege, regardless of what happens to the other fellow. They are gluttons of privilege. . . .

"How well you must remember the depression of the 1930s! The Republicans gave you that greatest of all depressions . . . when hogs went down to three cents and corn was so cheap you were burning it up. . . .

"[The] Republican Congress—that notorious 'do-nothing' Eightieth Congress—has already stuck a pitchfork in the farmer's back."

"These polls that the Republican candidate is putting out are like sleeping pills designed to lull the voters into sleeping on election day. You might call them sleeping polls."

The Republican doctrine, according to Truman:
"If you can't convince them, confuse them."

"I hope you will listen to my speech tonight [October 11, 1948] in Akron. I'm going to take the hide off 'em from top to bottom. I hate to have to do that, but they have it coming."

"The Republican party candidate said, and I quote him—now listen to this: 'I am proud of the record of my party and of the Eightieth Congress.' I just wonder what he has got to be proud of?

"And he said this, too—and I quote him again, 'The Eightieth Congress delivered as no other Congress ever did for the future of our country.'

"Well, I'll say it delivered. It delivered for the private power lobby. It delivered for the big oil company lobby. It delivered for the railroad lobby. It delivered for the real estate lobby. That's what the Republican candidate calls delivering for the future."

"Herbert Hoover once ran on the slogan, 'Two cars in every garage.' Apparently the Republican candidate this year is running on the slogan, 'Two families in every garage.' "

"In a prepared speech delivered in Phoenix, Arizona, the Republican candidate solemnly informed the people at Phoenix, and I quote, 'You know that your future is still ahead of you.' Exciting, don't you think? . . .

"At last I found an issue on which he was willing to take a position. But this position did remind me of [a] little verse . . . which goes something like this:

> 'Nothing here but the present,
> 'Nothing behind but the past,
> 'Nothing ahead but the future,
> 'My gosh, how long will it last?' "

"Wait until the morning of November 3 [the day after the 1948 election], and you are going to see more red-faced pollsters than you ever looked at in your life!"

On the morrow of Truman's remarkable victory:
"I am through giving them hell."

WAR AND PEACE

★ ★ ★

"Once in a while, I get a letter from some impatient person asking, why don't we get it over with? Why don't we issue an ultimatum [to Moscow], make all-out war, drop the atomic bomb?

"For most Americans, the answer is quite simple: We are not made that way. We are a moral people. Peace is our goal, with justice and freedom. We cannot, of our own free will, violate the very principles that we are striving to defend. The whole purpose of what we are doing is to prevent World War III. Starting a war is no way to make peace."

"Never in history has society been confronted with a power [of the atom] so full of potential danger and at the same time so full of promise for the future of man and for the peace of the world. I think I can express the faith of the American people when I say that we can use the knowledge we have won, not for the devastation of war but for the future welfare of humanity."

"Starting an atomic war is totally unthinkable for rational men."

"Faced with the terrible realities of the application of science to destruction, every nation will realize more urgently than before the overwhelming need to maintain the rule of law among nations and to banish the scourge of war from the earth."

"The atomic bombs which fell on Hiroshima and Nagasaki must be made a signal, not for the old process of falling apart, but for a new era—an era of ever-closer unity and ever-closer friendship among peaceful nations.

"Building a peace requires as much moral stamina as waging a war. Perhaps it requires even more, because it is so laborious and painstaking and undramatic. It requires undying patience and continuous application. But it can give us, if we stay with it, the greatest reward that there is in the whole field of human effort."

"The thought that frightens me is the possibility of the deliberate annihilation of whole peoples as a political–military objective. There were indications of such madness in the Nazi leadership group, and it could happen elsewhere. Terms of surrender have no meaning here. The only thing that does have meaning, and in all my thinking I have found no alternative, is organized international effort."

"The will for peace without the strength for peace is of no avail."

"It was the spirit of liberty which gave us our armed strength and which made our men invincible in battle. We now know that the spirit of liberty, the freedom of the individual, and the personal dignity of man are the strongest and toughest and most enduring forces in the world."

"There is profound truth in the first line of the ... charter of the United Nations Educational, Scientific, and Cultural Organization (UNESCO). The charter declares, 'Since wars begin in the minds of men, it is in the minds of men that the defenses of peace must be constructed.'

"I fear we are too much concerned with material things to remember that our real strength lies in spiritual values. I doubt whether there is in this troubled world today, when nations are divided by jealousy and suspicion, a single problem that could not be solved if approached in the spirit of the Sermon on the Mount.

"The new age of atomic energy presses upon us. Mark that well! What may have been sufficient yesterday is not sufficient today. New and terrible urgencies, new and terrible responsibilities, have been placed upon education.

"Ignorance and its handmaidens, prejudice, intolerance, suspicion of our fellow men, breed dictators. And they breed wars. Civilization cannot survive an atomic war. Nothing would be left but a world reduced to rubble. Gone would be man's hope for decency. Gone would be our hope for the greatest age in the history of mankind—an age which I know can harness atomic energy for the welfare of man and not for his destruction.

"And so we must look to education in the long run to wipe out that ignorance which threatens catastrophe. Intelligent men do not hate other men just because their religion may be different, or because their habits and language may be different, or because their national origin or color may be different. It is up to education to bring about that deeper international understanding which is so vital to world peace."

"We seek no territorial expansion or selfish advantage. We have no plans for aggression against any state, large or small. We have no objective which needs clash with the peaceful aims of any other nation."

"I [have] always been opposed to colonialism. Whatever justification may be cited at any stage, colonialism in any form is hateful to Americans. America fought her own war of liberation against colonialism, and we shall always regard with sympathy and understanding the desire of people everywhere to be free of colonial bondage."

"So long as I am president, the United States will not carry a chip on its shoulder."

"I am hoping that the United States of America can implement a foreign policy which will be the policy of the people of the United States and not the policy of any political party."

"It is no longer enough merely to say, 'We don't want war.' We must act in time—ahead of time—to stamp out the smoldering beginnings of any conflict that may threaten to spread over the world."

"We all have to recognize, no matter how great our strength, that we must deny ourselves the license to do always as we please. No one nation, no regional group, can or should expect any special privilege which harms any other nation. If any nation would keep security for itself, it must be ready and willing to share security with all. That is the price which each nation will have to pay for world peace. Unless we are all willing to pay that price, no organization for world peace can accomplish its purpose."

"Many of our people . . . used to think that we could escape the troubles of the world by simply staying within our own borders. Two [world] wars have shown us how wrong they were. We know today that we cannot find security in isolation. If we are to live in peace, we must join with other nations in a continuing effort to organize the world for peace. Science and invention have left us no other alternative."

"The Marshall Plan will go down in history as one of America's greatest contributions to the peace of the world. I think the world now realizes that without the Marshall Plan it would have been difficult for western Europe to remain free from the tyranny of communism."

"A just and lasting peace cannot be attained by diplomatic agreement alone, or by military cooperation alone. Experience has shown how deeply the seeds of war are planted by economic rivalry and by social injustice."

"The door has never been closed, nor will it ever be closed, to the Soviet Union or any other nation which will genuinely cooperate in preserving peace. . . .

"The United States has a tremendous responsibility to act according to the measure of our power for good in the world. We have learned that we must earn the peace we seek just as we earned victory in war, not by wishful thinking but by realistic effort."

"No American policy worthy of the name will ever treat any other nation as a satellite. It is basic to the way of life of democratic peoples that they respect the opinion of others, whether they happen to be weak or strong, rich or poor."

"I have been reading reports from many parts of the world. These reports all agree on one major point—the people of every nation are sick of war. They know its agony and its futility. No responsible government can ignore this universal feeling."

"There is something I would say to Stalin: You claim belief in Lenin's prophecy that one stage in the development of Communist society would be war between your world and ours. But Lenin was a pre-atomic man, who viewed society and history with pre-atomic eyes. Something profound has happened since he wrote. War has changed its shape and its dimension. It cannot now be a 'stage' in the development of anything save ruin."

"I have lived a long time and seen much happen in our country. And I know out of my own experience that we can do what must be done.

"When I think back to the country I grew up in, and then look at what our country has become, I am quite certain that, having done so much, we can do more.

"After all, it has been scarcely fifteen years since most Americans rejected out of hand the wise counsel [of President Franklin D. Roosevelt] that aggressors must be 'quarantined.' The very concept of collective security, the foundation stone of all our actions now, was then strange doctrine, shunned and set aside. Talk about adapting! Talk about adjusting! Talk about responding as a people to the challenge of changed times and circumstances! There never has been a more spectacular example than this great change in America's outlook on the world.

"Let all of us pause now, think back, consider carefully the meaning of our national experience. Let us draw comfort from it and faith and confidence in our future as Americans.

"The nation's business is never finished. The basic questions we have been dealing with these last eight years [1945–1953] present themselves anew. That is the way of our society. Circumstances change and current questions take on different forms, new complications, year by year. But underneath, the great issues remain the same: prosperity, welfare, human rights, effective democracy, and, above all, peace."

"A good many people in the world today seem to have lost their hope for peace and their courage to work for it. They seem to have forgotten that courage and the determination to stand up for what is right are essential if peace and liberty are to prevail. When they look around them, they see only trouble and danger. It is our job—the job of the American people—to help restore confidence all over the world that peace is not only possible but inevitable if the peoples of the world work together. It is our job to restore the courage of those who are so worried about today that they have lost the heart to work for tomorrow."

"Our nation has always been a land of great opportunities for those people of the world who sought to become part of us. Now we have become a land of great responsibilities to all the people of the world."

"I desire to do everything in my power to support and to contribute to a concert of all the forces striving for a moral world. Those forces are in the homes of peaceful and law-abiding citizens in every part of the world who are exemplifying in their own lives the principles of the good neighbor: the Golden Rule itself. They are on the farms, in the factories, mines, and little shops in all parts of the world where the principles of free cooperation and voluntary association in self-government are honored. These moral aspirations are in the hearts of good men the world over."

"There isn't any difference between Hitler and Mussolini [or] in the Tarquins of ancient Rome, in the Kings of Sparta, in Charles I of England, and Louis XIV—and Stalin. They are all just alike. Alexander I of Russia was just as much a dictator as any other that ever existed. They believed in the enslavement of the common people.

"This republic of ours has been founded on a different program. I think the greatest part of the Constitution is the Bill of Rights, and I believe that we should give everything we have to see that the Bill of Rights is maintained for the benefit of the individual. . . .

"If you go down through history, you will find that the fight has been to maintain the right to worship as we please, talk as we please, and act as we please, so long as we don't interfere with the rights of others. This has been the struggle down through the ages."

"There has never been a nation in the history of the world placed on a stronger foundation than ours. There has never been a nation in the history of the world as unselfish, and with the ideals that we believe in the welfare of every individual in the world as well as our own. There has never been a nation in the world which in time of victory has helped the vanquished to recover, as we have. I don't think you will find a situation like that anywhere in the history of the world."

"Some of you may ask, when and how will the cold war end. I think I can answer that simply. The Communist world has great resources, and it looks strong. But there is a fatal flaw in their society. Theirs is a godless system, a system of slavery; there is no freedom in it, no consent. The Iron Curtain, the secret police, the constant purges, all these are symptoms of a great basic weakness— the rulers' fear of their own people.

"In the long run the strength of our free society and our ideals will prevail over a system that has respect for neither God nor man. . . .

"As the free world grows stronger, more united, more attractive to men on both sides of the Iron Curtain and as Soviet hopes for easy expansion are blocked, then there will have to come a time of change in the Soviet world. Nobody can say for sure when that is going to be, or exactly how it will come about, whether by revolution, or trouble in the satellite states, or by a change inside the Kremlin.

"Whether the Communist rulers shift their policies of their own free will, or whether the change comes about in some other way, I have not a doubt in the world that a change will occur.

"I have a deep and abiding faith in the destiny of free men."

"With patience and courage, we shall some-day move on into a new era—a wonderful golden era—an age when we can use the peaceful tools that science has forged for us to do away with poverty and human misery everywhere on earth. . . .

"The Tigris and Euphrates Valley can be made to bloom as it did in the times of Babylon and Nineveh. Israel can be made the country of milk and honey as it was in the times of Joshua.

"There is a plateau in Ethiopia some six thousand to eight thousand feet high that has 65,000 square miles of land just exactly like the cornbelt in northern Illinois. Enough food can be raised there to feed a hundred million people.

"There are places in South America—places in Colombia and Venezuela and Brazil—just like that plateau in Ethiopia—places where food could be raised for millions of people.

"These things can be done. . . . This is our dream of the future."

"Peace is precious to us. It is the way of life we strive for with all the strength and wisdom we possess. But more precious than peace are freedom and justice. We will fight, if fight we must, to keep our freedom and to prevent justice from being destroyed."

Statement by the President Announcing the Use of the A-Bomb at Hiroshima

Sixteen hours ago an American airplane dropped one bomb on Hiroshima, an important Japanese Army base. That bomb had more power than twenty thousand tons of TNT. It had more than two thousand times the blast power of the British "Grand Slam," which is the largest bomb ever yet used in the history of warfare.

The Japanese began the war from the air at Pearl Harbor. They have been repaid many fold. And the end is not yet. With this bomb we have now added a new and revolutionary increase in destruction to supplement the growing power of our armed forces. In their present form these bombs are now in production and even more powerful forms are in development.

It is an atomic bomb. It is a harnessing of the basic power of the universe. The force from which the sun draws its power has been loosed against those who brought war to the Far East.

Before 1939, it was the accepted belief of scientists that it was theoretically possible to release atomic energy. But no one knew any practical method of doing it. By 1942, however, we knew that the Germans were working feverishly to find a way to add atomic energy to the other engines of war with which they hoped to enslave the world. But they failed. We may be grateful to Providence that the Germans got the V-1's and V-2's late and in limited quantities and even more grateful that they did not get the atomic bomb at all.

The battle of the laboratories held fateful risks for us as well as the battles of the air, land, and sea, and we have now won the battle of the laboratories as we have won the other battles.

Beginning in 1940, before Pearl Harbor, scientific knowledge useful in war was pooled between the United States and Great Britain, and many priceless helps to our victories have come from that arrangement. Under that general policy the research on the atomic bomb was begun. With American and British scientists working together we entered the race of discovery against the Germans.

The United States had available the large number of scientists of distinction in the many needed areas of knowledge. It had the tremendous industrial and financial resources necessary for the project and they could be devoted to it without undue impairment of other vital war work. In the United States the laboratory work and the production plants, on which a substantial start had already been made, would be out of reach of enemy bombing, while at that time Britain was exposed to constant air attack and was still threatened with the possibility of invasion. For these reasons Prime Minister Churchill and President Roosevelt agreed that it was wise to carry on the project here. We now have two great plants and many lesser works devoted to the production of atomic power. Employment during peak construction numbered 125,000 and over 65,000 individuals are even now engaged in operating the plants. Many have worked there for two and a half years. Few know what they have been producing. They see great quantities of material going in and they see nothing coming out of these plants, for the physical size of the explosive charge is exceedingly small. We have spent two billion dollars on the greatest scientific gamble in history—and won.

But the greatest marvel is not the size of the enterprise, its secrecy, nor its cost, but the achievement of scientific brains in putting together infinitely complex pieces of knowledge held by many men in different fields of science into a workable plan. And hardly less marvelous has been the capacity of industry to design, and of labor to operate, the machines and methods to do things never done before, so that the brainchild of many minds came forth in physical shape and performed as it was supposed to do. Both science and industry worked under the direction of the United States Army, which achieved a unique success in managing so diverse a problem in the advancement of knowledge in an amazingly short time. It is doubtful if such another combination could be got together in the world. What has been done is the greatest achievement of organized science in history. It was done under high pressure and without failure.

We are now prepared to obliterate more rapidly and completely every productive enterprise the Japanese have above ground in any city. We shall destroy their docks, their factories, and their communications. Let there be no mistake; we shall completely destroy Japan's power to make war.

It was to spare the Japanese people from utter destruction that the ultimatum of July 26 was issued at Potsdam. Their leaders promptly rejected that ultimatum. If they do not now accept our terms they may expect a rain of ruin from the air, the like of which has never been seen on this earth. Behind this air attack will follow sea and land forces in such numbers and power as they have not yet seen and with the fighting skill of which they are already well aware.

The Secretary of War, who has kept in personal touch with all phases of the project, will immediately make public a statement giving further details.

His statement will give facts concerning the sites at Oak Ridge near Knoxville, Tennessee, and at Richland near Pasco, Washington, and an installation near Santa Fe, New Mexico. Although the workers at the sites have been making materials to be used in producing the greatest destructive force in history, they have not themselves been in danger beyond that of many other occupations, for the utmost care has been taken of their safety.

The fact that we can release atomic energy ushers in a new era in man's understanding of nature's forces. Atomic energy may in the future supplement the power that now comes from coal, oil, and falling water, but at present it cannot be produced on a basis to compete with them commercially. Before that comes there must be a long period of intensive research.

It has never been the habit of the scientists of this country or the policy of this government to withhold from the world scientific knowledge. Normally, therefore, everything about the work with atomic energy would be made public.

But under present circumstances it is not intended to divulge the technical processes of production or all the military applications, pending further examination of possible methods of protecting us and the rest of the world from the danger of sudden destruction.

I shall recommend that the Congress of the United States consider promptly the establishment of an appropriate commission to control the production and use of atomic power within the United States. I shall give further consideration and make further recommendations to the Congress as to how atomic power can become a powerful and forceful influence towards the maintenance of world peace.

This statement was released in Washington. It was drafted before the President left Germany, and Secretary of War Stimson was authorized to release it when the bomb was delivered.

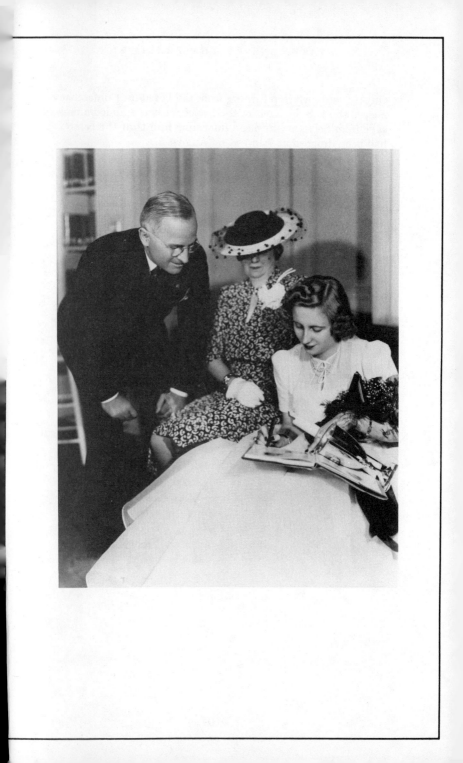

On August 6, while returning from the Potsdam Conference aboard the U.S.S. *Augusta*, the President was handed a message from Secretary Stimson informing him that the bomb had been dropped at 7:15 P.M. on August 5.

CHRONOLOGY

1884

May 8   Born in Lamar, Missouri, to John Anderson Truman and Martha Ellen Young Truman.

1885

May 1   Family moved to Cass County, Missouri, where Truman's father ran a farm.

1887

March   Family moved to Grandview, Missouri, to the farm of Truman's maternal grandfather, Sol Young.

1890

December 12   Family moved to Independence, Missouri.

1901

June   Graduated from Independence High School, having previously attended the Nolan School and the Columbian School.

September 15   Took a temporary job as a timekeeper on the Atcheson, Topeka & Santa Fe Railroad.

1902

August 10   Employed in the mail room of the *Kansas City Star* at $7 a week.

October   In Kansas City, worked for the National Bank of Commerce and later for the Union National Bank.

1905

January 16   Joined Battery B, Missouri National Guard, in Kansas City as a private.

1906

> **January** Returned to Grandview to work on the family farm for the next ten years.

1909

> **February 9** Received his first degree in the Masonic Order, Belton Lodge No. 450 at Belton, Missouri. Three months later he received his third degree in the Masonic Order.

1914

> **November 15** Named road overseer of Washington Township, Missouri, a post that had been held by his late father.

1915

> **April 1** Appointed postmaster of Grandview at $50 a month.

1916

> **September 25** Invested $5,000 in the Atlas-Okla Oil Lands Syndicate and became treasurer of the new firm, which went out of business when the United States entered the First World War in 1917.

1918

> **March 30** Now a first lieutenant, Truman sailed from New York for France on the troopship *George Washington*.

> **July 11** Placed in command of Battery D, 129th Field Artillery, 35th Division, in France, and saw his first action in the Vosges Mountains on September 6. Subsequently participated in the fighting at the Meuse-Argonne and Verdun.

1919

May 6   Discharged as a captain from the army at Camp Funsten, Kansas.

June 28   At the age of thirty-five, married Elizabeth (Bess) Virginia Wallace in Trinity Episcopal Church in Independence.

November 29   Opened a haberdashery in Kansas City with his partner, Edward Jacobson. Prospering at first, the venture failed in the depression of 1920–1921. Shunning bankruptcy, Truman paid off his debts over a period of years.

1922

November 4   Supported by the Pendergast Democratic organization, Truman was elected a judge (commissioner) of Jackson County, Missouri.

1924

February 17   Daughter, Mary Margaret, born in Kansas City.

November 6   Ran again for county commissioner and suffered the only election defeat of his career.

1925

January 7   Employed by the Automobile Club of Kansas City.

1926

November 2   Elected presiding commissioner of Jackson County, a post he held until he was elected a United States senator from Missouri on November 5, 1934.

1935
  January 3   Sworn in as a senator by Vice-President
                     John Nance Garner.

1940
  November 5   Reelected senator.

1941
  February 17   Appointed chairman of the Senate Special
                     Committee to Investigate the National
                     Defense Program (known as the Truman
                     Committee).

1944
  July 21   Nominated by the Democratic National
                     Convention as vice-president to run with
                     President Franklin D. Roosevelt in the
                     latter's quest for a fourth term.

  November 7   Roosevelt and Truman defeated the Repub-
                     lican ticket of Thomas E. Dewey and John
                     W. Bricker.

1945
  January 20   Inaugurated as vice-president.
  April 12   Sworn in as president of the United States
                     by Chief Justice Harlan F. Stone in the
                     White House, at 7:09 P.M., hours after the
                     sudden death of Roosevelt at Warm Springs,
                     Georgia.

  May 8   Informed the nation of the unconditional
                     surrender of Germany.

  July 17–   Attended the Potsdam Conference in Ger-
  August 2   many with leaders of Great Britain and
                     the Soviet Union.

August 6   Received the word of the dropping of the atomic bomb on Hiroshima, an attack which he had ordered.

August 15   Announced the surrender of Japan.

1946
May 24   Threatened to draft railroad strikers into the army to run the trains.

1947
January 6   Delivered the State of the Union Message to the Eightieth Congress, in which Republicans had captured control of both houses.

March 12   Delivered the Truman Doctrine speech to Congress, asking for $400 million to defend Greece and Turkey against the danger of Communist control.

June 5   The program that came to be known as the Marshall Plan was broached to the public by Secretary of State George C. Marshall in the commencement address at Harvard University.

1948
May 15   Truman extended de facto recognition to the new State of Israel.

June 24   Ordered an airlift to counter the Soviet blockade of Berlin.

November 2   Scored the most sensational upset in American political history by winning a second term, defeating the heavily favored Thomas Dewey. In the historic election, four parties were in the race, including the Progressive Party, whose candidate was former vice-president Henry A. Wallace, and the

States' Rights Democrats (Dixiecrats) led by Governor J. Strom Thurmond of South Carolina.

1949

January 5   Launched his second term with a State of the Union Message outlining a program dubbed the Fair Deal, essentially calling for extension and expansion of the New Deal of Franklin Roosevelt.

April 4   The North Atlantic Treaty was signed in Washington.

September 23   Truman announced that the Soviet Union had exploded a nuclear device, ending the American monopoly on the atomic bomb.

October 1   Mao Zedong proclaimed the People's Republic of China, bringing China under the Communist banner.

1950

January 31   Truman decided that the United States would build a hydrogen bomb.

June 24 (Washington time)   Communist-controlled North Korea invaded American-supported South Korea.

June 26   Truman committed U.S. air and naval forces to the support of South Korea.

June 28   Appointed General of the Army Douglas A. MacArthur head of American (and later United Nations) forces in Korea.

June 30   Committed ground forces to battle in Korea.

October 14   Conferred on the Korean War with MacArthur on Wake Island after United Nations forces had begun crossing the 38th parallel into North Korea to crush the North Korean army.

November 1	Escaped assassination as two Puerto Rican nationalists tried to shoot their way into Blair House, where the Trumans were living while the White House was undergoing renovation.
November 28	Notified by MacArthur that the Chinese Communists had entered the Korean War in great force in support of North Korea and were hurling United Nations forces back toward South Korea.
December 15	Announced that he would proclaim a national emergency because of the Korean War.

1951

January 1	Chinese Communist offensive recaptures Seoul, the South Korean capital.
April 11	Truman relieved MacArthur of his command in Korea because of insubordination and the general's unwillingness to see the war limited to Korea instead of expanded to include air and naval bombardment of Communist China.
July 10	Korean cease-fire talks opened after United Nations forces repulsed the North Korean advance into South Korea.

1952

March 29	Truman announced at a Jefferson–Jackson Day dinner in Washington that he would not be a candidate for reelection in November.
July 25	With Truman's backing, Governor Adlai E. Stevenson of Illinois won the Democratic presidential nomination.

November 4   Eisenhower and his running mate, Richard M. Nixon, elected in a landslide.

1953
January 20   Truman's term ended.

1956
April 21   Attended the wedding of his daughter, Margaret, to Clifton Daniel of the *New York Times.*

1957
July 7   Harry S Truman Library, in Independence, Missouri, dedicated.

1958
February 19   Truman accepted the position of Chubb Fellow at Yale University.

1959
April 13   Began his lecture series on the presidency at Columbia University.

1964
May 9   Addressed the Senate, becoming the first former president to address that body while in formal session.

1966
January 21   President Lyndon B. Johnson presented Medicare Card #1 to Truman in Independence, in recognition of the fact that Truman had been the first to propose a system similar to Medicare.

1972
December 26   Truman died in a Kansas City hospital.

SOURCES

The quotations in this book were selected from the speeches, statements, letters, diaries, press conferences, and memoirs of Harry S Truman, and can be found in the following volumes.

Conflict and Crisis: The Presidency of Harry S Truman, 1945–1948, by Robert J. Donovan (New York: W. W. Norton and Company, 1977).

Dear Bess: The Letters from Harry S Truman to Bess Truman, 1910–1959, edited by Robert H. Ferrell (New York: W. W. Norton & Company, 1983).

Memoirs by Harry S Truman: Years of Decisions (New York: Doubleday and Company, 1955).

Memoirs by Harry S Truman: Years of Trial (New York: Doubleday and Company, 1956).

Mr. Citizen (New York: Popular Library, 1953).

Mr. Presiи̃ent (New York: Farrar, Straus and Young, 1952).

Off the Record: The Private Papers of Harry S Truman, edited by Robert H. Ferrell (New York: Harper & Row, 1980).

Public Papers of the Presidents of the United States: Harry S Truman (Washington, D.C.: U. S. Government Printing Office). These cover eight official volumes, cited by year.

Truman Speaks (New York: Columbia University Press, 1975).

Tumultuous Years: The Presidency of Harry S Truman, 1949–1953, by Robert J. Donovan (New York: W. W. Norton & Company, 1982).

The photographs in this book are from the following sources:

p. 2: Harry S Truman; photo by Leo Stern, courtesy Harry S Truman Library and Museum.

p. 18: Vice-President Truman with Lauren Bacall at the National Press Club canteen, Washington, D. C., February 10, 1945; courtesy AP/Wide World Photos.

p. 24: Senator Truman on the rostrum after his nomination as vice-president by the Democratic National Convention, July 21, 1944; courtesy AP/Wide World Photos.

p. 32: Truman walks along a dock at the U.S. Naval Base at Key West, March 23, 1951; courtesy UPI.

p. 36: Truman and Vice-President Barkley after their inauguration, January 20, 1949; courtesy Harry S Truman Library and Museum.

p. 38: Ex-president Truman gets in line to purchase a newspaper in Union Terminal, Cincinnati, as his train makes a stopover enroute to Independence, Missouri, January 21, 1953; courtesy AP/Wide World Photos.

p. 44: Truman taking the oath of office of the presidency at the White House after the death of Franklin D. Roosevelt, April 12, 1945; at his side are his wife, Bess, and daughter, Margaret; courtesy National Park Services.

p. 46: Truman is silhouetted by the early-morning sun as he walks along the square in Independence, Missouri, August 14, 1961; courtesy AP/Wide World Photos.

p. 52: Truman delivers his first address to the nation as president, before a joint session of Congress, April 16, 1945; courtesy Harry S Truman Library and Museum.

p. 60: Truman holding the incorrectly headlined *Chicago Tribune* newspaper, November 3, 1948; courtesy *St. Louis Globe-Democrat*.

p. 68: Reporters jam the room as Truman holds his regular news conference in the executive offices building, April 3, 1952; courtesy AP/Wide World Photos.

p. 72: Truman at his desk in the reproduction of the oval office at the Harry S Truman Library and Museum in Independence, Missouri, 1959; courtesy Harry S Truman Library and Museum.

p. 78: Truman announces the surrender of Germany, May 8, 1945; courtesy AP/Wide World Photos.

p. 88: Truman and General Douglas A. MacArthur, 1950; U.S. Army photo, courtesy Harry S Truman Library and Museum.

p. 102: The Truman family; photo by Heller, courtesy Harry S Truman Library and Museum.